Chris Leo

8 HABITS OF THE RICH

Wealth Secrets That Will

Make You Consistently Rich

First Published May 2023
Republished February 2024

Chris Leo

© Palace Media 2024

All Rights Reserved

TABLE OF CONTENT

CONCLUSION

INTRODUCTION

Denis began consulting within the finance industry some 25 years ago and he related with rich customers from a range of diverse backgrounds. He consulted for big financial institutions across the USA and Europe, and had dealings with a few wealthy business people from Africa and Asia.

He worked with pacesetters of industries, including owners of superstores, product manufacturers, and bookkeeping multinationals. These people are the top one percent of the customer base he worked. Denis shared the eight mannerisms these few people have in common.

Denis' experience in the financial field spanned over 35 years. He made tremendous impact in his hometown of Houston and everywhere he sojourned within those years. Recently, after reading my book, *7 Wealth Habits To Free You From Poverty*, he obliged to share his experiences with the rich and affluent with me.

As my tradition, sharing experiences of greatness and goodness that can lift people from low life to top life gives me joy. I want to see people grow out of ignorance into all-round sound knowledge. Hence, this book is a catalogue of few things he shared with me.

Not everyone seems to understand how the wealthy makes wealth seamlessly. It appears to be their destiny to live in super affluence. However, you must admit that these people do not all believe in destiny but sheer diligence, daring faith, dexterity and desire to make their lives better.

The world sees some of them as self-made rich men because of this strong belief, which is common to them. If you are a religious mind, you may not like their way unless you position yourself where you can view life from their perspectives.

Riches and wealth can come to anyone but a few potentials, practices, and procedures are common to all wealthy people. You cannot break into that caliber until you know those habits, approaches and observe them meticulously.

Some of the things you will read in this book may be new to you. If come you come across any facts that are not new, do not flip but dutifully read between the lines. You will unmask hidden facts that can turn you into a 7-figure earner in no distant time. Therefore, I encourage you to read every page of this book as many times as possible until the message sinks and the lessons begin to reflect in your daily lifestyle.

At any point, if you face challenges that want to keep you down, remember these words: It is a hard way to be rich. It is also a hard way to be poor; however, you must choose your hard way! Rich or poor – it all depends on that choice. To your wealth and success!

Chris Leo

HABIT ONE

Time Consciousness

Their time is their most precious asset. Time is money.

Super prosperous people do not waste their time in undertakings that do not profit them. To them, there is no use embarking on activities that have no cash value and cannot attract fulfilment to them. They consider it sheer waste of resources doing something with their time that cannot add financial value or result in financial reality.

Time is the decisive currency. The entire purpose of pursuing a course is to get back time. Some people do this by keeping some resources aside for retirement. The rich people do it so they can do what they want, at any time they want, and however they choose.

Denis once shared this. "I had an appointment for 10.00 a.m. with the president of a group of companies. His company provided services in over 80 locations in Texas alone, and over 500 stores located across the United States.

Due to some issues that came up that morning, I could not leave for the office early enough. On the way, I had called my secretary to find out when the man arrived there. It was 5 minutes to 10a.m. by the time I arrived at my office, it was 10.06a.m, and the man had left.

The 6 minutes was too much of a delay for him to bear, hence he left just before I got there. In my candid view, it was somehow extreme. I concluded that he was not patient and that he was full of self-importance. However, I learnt later in life that it was that habit that kept him on top."

Like Denis, you may feel that it is extreme of rich people to show impatience. You may even think it is pride or an attitude to show off, but to him, it is a matter of maximizing his asset. Time indeed is an asset. It seems only the rich people understand it that way.

Moreover, it is common among people that work constantly and schedule each second of their day to act that way. You should not blame them because experience has taught them to take time serious in every transaction. If you cannot respect and keep an agreement time with someone, it is likely that you will fail in keeping other valuable assets such as money.

Dr. Charles is a medical doctor-turned-entrepreneur. He was about 62 years when I first spoke with him. That was two years ago. We met and connected online. I love his ideologies and follow most of his online publications. He is rather an unusual man considering his age and education. Some people regard him as abnormal personality and he never denied being himself.

When I contacted him for a session on very important issues of my life and career, he obliged and sent his two direct telephone numbers. That humbled me. He asked me to call on a particular day by 10.00a.m. It was a Friday.

By 9.58a.m, I dialed his number. Due to network issues, I decided to put a call across 2 minutes before the time and by exactly 10 O'clock, it went through and he picked the call. His first statement was, "Chris, you are a good man. Now, I can talk with you."

We had a wonderful conversation and he went beyond my expectation to grant me some valuable ideas on succeeding in my career. This man delivers lectures and seminars on entrepreneurship across Africa, Europe, and Asia and has associates all over the US and the UK. Time is key to opening special doors to great minds.

HABIT 2

Strong Bargaining Power

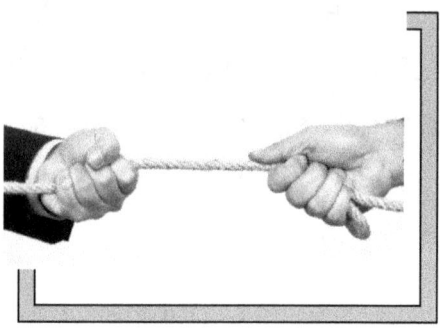

They are great negotiators. They apparently seem to understand the word "bargain" more than any other person does. The first offer is never good enough. The rich believes that the price can still go down so they negotiate.

These men are swift thinkers, self-assured, and stretch their status. This can intimidate you at first, but the more quickly you realize that this is part of the strategies of being rich, the more you lean towards their lifestyle.

Denis expressed some of the questions they used to ask him. Almost all of them have this sense of strong bargaining power.

One would remark, "The rate on savings account is not high enough. Can you get the bank to take precedence over it and deliver something higher?"

Another would observe, "The interest rate on my real estate loan is too high. Can you get the bank to adjust the rate? If you don't mind, I can get something lower elsewhere."

This is what happens when you attain an appreciable level of wealth. It should also be a motivation to strive to get there if you are still struggling at the low level. The rich do not care about the profits of the company they deal with, they are only after their own gain. This is why they drive hard bargains.

If they do not get a good fee on their account, they are ready to move to where they can get it. If the financial institution charge them high on their account, they would not mind going to some other banks where they do not charge that much. All they seek constantly is a waiver. They never give up until they get it. This is an attitude that keeps them consistently rich.

They are always aiming at the very best in terms of bargains and negotiations. They know their right and fight for it without offending the other party. Moreover, their partners whether individuals or corporate firms accord them their dues and respect.

It appears the world of business favors people with this attitude. This could be so considering the value they have to offer. When you know what you have and can offer, and stand your ground in communicating it to those you deal with, you stand the chance to earn their trust, respect and the right to earn the royalty you demand.

If you show instability at the negotiation table, you may likely get less that the person who stands resolute in his demands for better deals. This attitude of the rich is quite ingenious and worthy of emulation.

HABIT 3

Value Little Earnings

The author of *Multiple Streams of Income,* Robert G. Allen said, "Every dollar bill is a money seed". That is, every cent earned is a soldier in the battle to end poverty and build a strong financial future. Meaning, you can end being broke in life.

Truly, every penny matters too. No rich person got to his current position of wealth by letting go of little things. They never let business opportunities slide. It is a matter of grabbing them and turning them into fortunes.

Most of the poor people you have probably met are chance-losers. They want to make it big but feel big to start small. This is a show of lack of humility and appreciation of the laws of nature. Everything grows from a tiny cell to a large organ. The mustard seed is tiny in nature but mighty in structure when matured.

David Feldman's book, *Small By Design* has so much to teach about this humble attitude of the rich people. You do not become big by starting big. You must develop a minimalist mindset while aiming to become big. To hit it financially big requires that you practice your swinging well before throwing the punch.

Even the wisest men know that rising in life is about taking advantage of the opportunities they meet at the bottom. When climbing the ladder of wealth, one of the rules is that you do not skip a rung in order to get to the top fast. The little things you will see on that journey or flight can either sustain you at the top or take you back to the previous level.

Imagine getting to a point in life only to realize so late that the little things that you neglected were capable of launching you into bigtime wealth. Most people who live in regret today became oblivious of the little steps to super riches. They never knew that excellent financial breakthrough hide in some insignificant opportunities. You must not let your later life experience such regrets.

"Little by little, says the thoughtful boy. Moment by moment, I will implore."

The first two lines of this nursery rhyme usually inspire me. Perhaps, you should look at them carefully. One or two lessons to help you be on the lookout for the next little opportunity to make an income no matter how little. I do not know the author of this rhyme but I reserve great respect for such a fellow. Possibly, he was a rich person.

8 Habits of the Rich

HABIT 4

Selective Association

They do not flock with just everyone. They are selective of who they mingle with in life. Not everyone is right for them. They look before they leap into any relationship. Check it out; their friends are equally wealthy.

Business holders hang out with other business holders. The rich hang out with the rich. That saying, birds of the same feathers flock together is probably for them. Like eagles, they do not flock with hawks or crows even though they are all flying animals.

The reason is simple; the people you hang out with vary your views, modify your motivation, and build your behaviors. Show me your friend and I will tell you who you are means more than an old saying to the rich. They actually make it their guide in relationship.

Just as addicts spend time with other addicts, the rich associate themselves with people of like-minds. This helps them not to derail from their goals and path to higher levels.

Once, a very important personality invited me for a chat in his house. At that time, I was trying to launch out into full-time career pursuit. This man was already a manager in a government agency in charge of social trust fund. He was a six-figure earner and was always giving talks on human resource management to some local bank staffs and inductees of corporations.

At first, I wondered why he invited someone like me who was not on his level of "wealth". During our chat that lasted for about 45 minutes, yeah, 45 long minutes, he told me something that changed my mindset about myself and how the rich thinks. These men and women have eyes that do not see the usual; they perceive wealth from a distance and consciously draw towards it.

To become rich, you must develop your mind to be visionary, to see what has not happened, to believe what your mind sees. The rich sees and smells greatness in people and then position themselves to connect when the time is right. This is what I realized after quite some time.

I was wondering why some people would break their long-standing principles once they met me. A one-time administrator of a big human resources organization welcomed me into his office. It was my first time there on an appointment. I had asked for his contribution to my first book series and he had invited me to talk about it.

The first message that greeted my eyes was a boldly written information, which said, "If you have spent 10 minutes in this office, you have overstayed your welcome. I did not know whether to think about my concern or his caution on the wall of his office.

I quickly started the conversation and by the 9th minute, I had completed my mission and was ready to leave. However, he was not through with me. Although I consistently showed that my time was up, this executive continued to entertain me with tons of quality counsel and shares of his experiences. By the time he was through, I realized we had spent more than 30 minutes chatting."

Few years later, I organized a free youth empowerment program and invited him as the special guest speaker. He drove several kilometers with his wife and two kids to the venue. This great man later expressed how he was seeing in me the great wealth potentials. It humbled me, yet taught me a great lesson on the compatibility theory.

You may be wondering why some poor people relocate to regions with mostly rich people once they become rich. It is because of this compatibility theory. Some people feel it is pride or just to show off their wealth. Not really. It is because the law of attraction comes into effect once you attain a level of wealth and honor.

If you do not think and see like these rich men, you would never attract them into your life. That means your association may end with only average people. Hence, to get into highways of wealth, you must drive your mindset to queue behind the company of the rich. It is a matter of time, what they have begins to flow to your direction.

In addition, whatever you set as your goal, do these:

❖ Connect with people already doing what you dream to do
❖ Cultivate a network of people with the kind of mindset

❖ Create good environment for accountability to one another

Build a team with them and keep growing it until you get to a point where members are strong enough to carry the responsibility of others who might become weak along the way.

Synergy is spreadable. It is like a contagious concept. The people you connect with control part of your practices sometimes unknowing to you. Hence, you should surround yourself with people who reflect how rich you want to be and how comfortable you want to feel.

HABIT 5

Strong Sense of Self

There is big difference between self-love and selfishness. You should be selfless in your service to humanity, but when it comes to self-service, you should try to be self-concerned. Self-love is key to selflessness!

Denis revealed, "In the course of my career and meeting these rich folks, I observed one more thing: They worry about themselves and no one else." This strong habit provides a wall of defense around these people. It becomes very difficult to penetrate them without their willingness to open up.

To worry about your own goals is a task big enough for you. Hence, letting someone else's ambition to bother you is not a wise choice. The rich understand that competing with others is a colossal waste of energy and time. They do not have that time to worry about the status of others but focus on their goals and targets.

It may seem they are selfish but that is not the case. It is simply about following the rules of taking charge of your life, having self-control, taking full responsibility for yourself, and doing your best to provide solution to your own problems. Therefore, it is about self-development and this requires all of yourself to achieve.

Self-growth and development promotes the following benefits, which you could call SARS. They are:

a. Strategy: Instead of bothering about someone's goals, you get busy mapping out smarter ways to push your own aspirations towards maturity.

b. Accountability: You tend to take regular stock of your activities when you focus more on yourself than on others. Becoming your own accountant is the best way to check your excesses, terminate frivolity and even mitigate abuse of every other resource available to you.

c. Resilience: the pursuit of your wealth targets requires doggedness and the never-give-up spirit. As you think more of yourself, you discover possible areas where you easily relapse. Then, you resolve to push harder until you achieve success in those areas. The rich mind is a resilient mind.

d. Success: Ultimately, this is the result of all your self-growth and development. No better result than success at the end of all you do. The more you develop yourself, the more success you record, and the more you inch towards wealthy status.

In the meantime, you will fail to achieve these values when you focus on others more than you do on yourself. Comparing yourself to some other persons will only drain you of the energy to do your own thing. Rich people do not allow themselves fooled into such unnecessary act.

HABIT 6

Fear No Failure

Fear is a natural response to the unknown. However, it is a big destroyer of good prospects. The rich people do not fear failure. This is because they have all failed greatly and do not let this worry them.

To them, failure is a learning experience. The inventor of light bulb failed to get it many times but he did not consider them as failures. Instead, he described them as experiments that never produced the result he expected. They were part of the process that birthed the ultimate discovery we all enjoy and celebrate today.

Although failure is not a reflection of self-worth, intelligence, or aptitude, yet it is part of being an enterprising person. Tackling new problems and trying something different may result in chances of failure. However, it does not show that you are not on the right track neither are you on a disaster-bound trip.

If you study the life of Mark Cuban for example, you will discover that failure is an asset in disguise. This man stands out as one of the best-known corporate business executives in the world. His net worth is about US$4.7 billion. Yet, he has a catalogue of failed experiences.

When he first graduated from college and began to work, he lost his first three employments. Then, he ventured into business and opened a bar. Not long after, he shut it down. He started a factory that produced powered milk. That one closed down due to bankruptcy.

In all that period, most people did not bother or even know about his failures. Among those that knew, some would have doubted his choice of business as a career. However, one thing kept him pushing on - the spirit of entrepreneurship in him. What his doggedness in spite of his numerous failures did was to provide valuable lessons for future business engagements.

These lessons taught Mark, as they teach every other wealthy person in business the following:

1. Making money is an unemotional endeavor.

If you are an entrepreneur, you must learn to detach from certain sentiments that are injurious to your overall quest to succeed. They do not let feelings get in the way of transactions. The deal is either good or bad. They will not do you a favor just because they can or that you feel deserving of it. There must be an exchange of values for them to do such favors.

You should learn that business is business. It is about facts and choices, statistics and solutions. Nothing more matters. The rest is the result, which hangs on the aforementioned.

2. Making money is entirely a personal task.

The rich do not hire family and friends. Any family member you find within their businesses has great value to offer and is someone who is not biased. It is an established fact that most close relatives ruin businesses given to them to run. They often treat the business with nonchalance and levity because it belongs to their relative. Instead, they employ the finest and most suitable persons they find to manage their company.

3. Making wealth is not for the fainthearted.

If you must win, you must settle it in your heart to stake all you have on it. The rich develop a solid shock absorber that sucks in pressures to quit. Imagine losing millions of dollars in a single transaction. Imagine closing down a business and opening another one in matter of months. That implies the pain of the loss does not prevent the pleasure of engaging other opportunities.

8 Habits of the Rich

HABIT 7

Always Learning

Knowledge is key but application of it is superior. It guarantees your consistent move up the ladder of wealth. The rich never stop learning. They relentlessly learn and adapt to the ever-changing world.

The world of business and entrepreneurship, which the richest people belong to is highly competitive. What sets some apart at the top is what they know. This knowledge comes from various sources mostly from books. Hence, they read a lot.

Reading books, magazines, journals, and other knowledge materials is probably their number one hobby. They occupy their time with studying new things. They are always open to new ideas and glean so much of it from documents and data in books. The secondary thing that probably takes their time is sports such as badminton, golf, horse race and chess.

Denis also observed that most of these rich people spend time reading while on transit especially when they are on board a flight. While some of the passengers listen to music or play videos on their iPhone and iPad respectively, this super rich class enjoys the company of good books. These books on economy, politics, foreign markets, international relations, etc. keep them informed on where their next big break could be waiting.

I read about the conversation between Bill Gates and his daughter. The daughter had called him up after midnight to ask what he was doing. The rich man replied that she should know what he was doing. He was in the study reading, researching, assimilating, and brooding. Great men are always in the habit of knowing more than they know. In fact, you should covet this one habit if you dream wealth like no other.

It is on record that Warren Buffett reads about 800 pages a day. That is such a big deal. US rich man Bill Gates reads more than 50 books a year. That is not something that one can achieve overnight.

I was in a public lecture organized by a top celebrity magazine in Nigeria, West Africa in 2005. The event took place at the prestigious 5-star hotel in the largest commercial city of West Africa. I was there in company of a friend who was studying marketing in a state university.

A certain multi-billionaire in Africa delivered a lecture at the event. Among many things he said, one statement inspired me to invest quality time and money in books. He said, "I don't claim to understand a book until I have read it the 12th or 13th time." That sounded unbelievable. No wonder he was already a chief executive of a group of companies at age 35.

Asides being studious and savoring books for up-to-date information, the rich also watch boring television channels such as CNBC, CNN, and other investment channels.it is quite normal and the usual for them to be up to date on financial markets, foreign exchange, and other economic indicators.

This habit is one that makes ordinary or average persons to stand out. When you look at the way they organize and discipline themselves to achieve wealth, some of these traits will guide your current decision-making and resolution to pursue the same goals with tenacity and audacity.

HABIT 8

Crazy Faith

The question that most people ask when faced with opportunity that could land them in super wealth is, "What if it costs everything?", "What if I lose it all?"

Hardly do they ask, "What if I make it big?" At this point, you know someone who will eventually win. Most average persons fear this moment but the rich, through experience, know it is their time to exercise crazy faith.

The resolution in their heart is, "I am stepping out; I am taking the lead", "I am closing this deal".

When the chips are down, the rich keeps investing. When the rate is low, they go ahead and buy up every cent of shares they can find. They know that a time will come when the prices will go up and they make crazy returns after sales.

One thing is responsible for this – crazy faith! A faith that dares the impossible. A faith that shows up at the negotiation table; that never takes No for an answer. A faith that turns the tide in their favor. The kind of faith you must have to break into the wealthy class.

The rich see the future before it arrives and by faith embrace it. They throw themselves into their trades in the hope of big returns on their investment. Even when others drag their feet, the rich stride and strive until they break into another level of wealth. Such unswerving faith is not common among the average persons; they usually want something on a platter and often never get it.

The rich hold the belief that no one gives you anything. You have to want it desperately and go for it. The world hardly gives what you desire or wish to have; you must learn to acquire it by a strong and stanch faith. Such is the mindset behind Barack Obama's Audacity of Hope. What you hope for, though not seen, yet you develop an audacious drive to acquire it.

Crazy faith is such that triumphs when the odds are clearly against you. It appears that you stand no chance in a thousand; yet by faith, you make the move that eventually sees you at the top of a million.

A friend of mine who lived many years in Spain got into trouble in Europe and the authorities deported him to his home country. When we met, he narrated how he lost over a million dollars, a casino that he just bought weeks before his problem began, plus all his household items that worth hundreds of thousands of dollars.

As he lamented his loss due to his misbehavior, he was still so optimistic of recovering all he had lost. He once bragged to me, "I made those monies; I can and will make them again." The expression on his face revealed a high degree of optimism and faith. Not even his then condition of lack could slow him down. He was so determined to move on to a better future.

Making money and maintaining the wealth status is not a task for a fainthearted person. It is not milk but strong meat. The courage to withstand unforeseen outcomes in business is what stands them out. The belief that they can rise above the storms associated with being rich and the spectacle of many keeps them on top. If you must walk that corridor for long, it is imperative that you develop crazy faith.

CONCLUSION

When you consider the lifestyle of the rich and affluent, and the habits so far listed, you will see that it takes serious work to rise to their level. Riches do not fly into an unprepared ground. There is always a preparation for wealth to nest in any area. Failure to make these preparations while striving to make money can lead to a huge waste of time and resources.

First, you must understand that habits drive hustles. Sound and positive habits can propel you to higher realms of success and riches. Once you get it right, the rest will be your success story. If otherwise, you may gather the money but lose it all due to deficiency in noble habits to keep driving you forward.

Wealth is not an indigene of a particular geographical location. It is open to anyone who pays the right price and makes the often-compulsory sacrifices. Granted, some inherit wealth but for you, who may not have been that lucky or privileged, do not expect to get rich overnight. You must learn the ropes.

You must learn some important and intelligent things millionaires do every day to help grow their wealth. It begins with adopting the habits you have read in this book. One after another, you get to understand how to become what you dream.

The rich and wealthy consistently follow a routine until it becomes part of their lifestyle. Then, they no longer see it as something new or strange. When you allow these habits take complete control of your personality and psychology, you will begin to radiate the kind of light that attracts riches to you anywhere you go.

This radiation is the secret behind the super attraction of wealth that the rich experience. You cannot attract what you have not become. Human life is like a magnet that draws anything that makes it useful. If a magnet does not magnet or attract anything to itself, it becomes useless and good for nothing. The same with life.

What your life needs as complementary is wealth to bring out your real beauty. Your ultimate relevance remains trapped in you without the sufficient resources to display it. Becoming wealthy gives you the leverage to show your significance and make a strong statement of sound responsibility.

Therefore, to wrap this up, strive to become what will attract what you must be for the rest of your life. If a life of fulfilment that wealth generates is your dream. Do not stop at dreaming it but proceed to covet it. Consistently, you will become not just wealthy, but a solid reference in the circle of impactful personalities in your region.